CW01460461

JOHN GRISHAM

BIOGRAPHY

Exploring the Framed Victims of a Flawed Legal System and the Craft of Justice

{53 Unknown Facts About Legal Thriller Master John Grisham}

Morris Glisson

Copyright © 2024, Morris Glisson

All rights reserved. No part of this book may be reproduced, distributed, or transmitted in any form or by any means, including photocopying, recording, or other electronic or mechanical methods, without the prior written permission of the publisher, except in the case of brief quotations embodied in critical reviews and certain other noncommercial uses permitted by copyright law.

TABLE OF CONTENTS

INTRODUCTION

John Grisham: A Voice for Justice

"There is a hole in the criminal justice system. A black hole." -John Grisham

This stark statement from John Grisham himself encapsulates the driving force behind his prolific writing career. He isn't just a master storyteller who has captivated millions with his legal thrillers; he's a lawyer turned author who uses his platform to expose the injustices and systemic flaws plaguing the American legal system. His novels, often ripped from the headlines or inspired by his own experiences in the courtroom, delve into the dark underbelly of the law, exploring themes of corruption, wrongful convictions, and the fight for justice against all odds.

But what ignited this passion within him? What experiences shaped his worldview and fueled his desire to give a voice to the voiceless? This biography aims to uncover the answers, tracing the journey of John Grisham from a small-town boy in Mississippi to a literary giant and a champion for the wrongfully convicted.

From Courtroom to Bestseller List: The Making of John Grisham

Grisham's path to becoming a bestselling author was far from conventional. Before he penned legal thrillers that would dominate bestseller lists and become blockbuster movies, he was a young lawyer navigating the complexities of the courtroom. He witnessed firsthand the disparities in the legal system, the power imbalances, and the devastating consequences of wrongful convictions. These experiences, coupled with his deep-seated sense of justice, laid the foundation for his future writing.

This biography will explore the profound impact of Grisham's personal and professional background on his views of justice. We'll examine his childhood in the racially charged South, his early exposure to law and literature, and his years practicing law in Mississippi. By understanding his formative years and the challenges he faced, we can gain deeper insight into the themes that permeate his work.

Key Themes: Justice, Injustice, and the Power of Storytelling

Throughout his career, Grisham has consistently shone a light on the vulnerabilities of the legal system. He has tackled complex issues such as racial bias, corporate greed, and the plight of the innocent caught in the crosshairs of the law. This biography will examine these recurring themes, analyzing how Grisham weaves them into his narratives to create compelling stories that resonate with readers worldwide.

We will delve into his exploration of wrongful convictions, a topic that has become synonymous with his name. From his early novels like "A Time to Kill" to his recent nonfiction work "Framed," Grisham has tirelessly advocated for those who have been unjustly imprisoned. This biography will examine the real-life cases that have inspired his activism and the impact he has had on the fight for justice reform.

Ultimately, this biography will not only provide a comprehensive account of John Grisham's life and work but also explore the power of storytelling to effect change. It will examine how Grisham has used his platform to raise awareness about critical issues and inspire others to fight for a more just and equitable society.

CHAPTER 1:

EARLY LIFE AND INFLUENCES

Childhood in Mississippi

John Grisham's childhood was a study in contrasts. Born in Jonesboro, Arkansas, in 1955, his family soon migrated to the Mississippi Delta, a region steeped in complex history, marked by both its vibrant culture and the lingering shadows of racial segregation. Growing up in Southaven, Mississippi, in the 1960s, young Grisham experienced firsthand the stark realities of a society grappling with social change. While his family wasn't directly involved in the Civil Rights struggles that were roiling the South, the atmosphere of inequality and injustice permeated the air he breathed.

9

This environment undoubtedly left an indelible mark on the young Grisham. He witnessed the disparities between Black and white communities, the subtle and overt forms of discrimination, and the simmering tensions that often erupted into violence. These early exposures to social injustice planted the seeds of his future concern with legal and moral issues, themes that would later dominate his writing.

Furthermore, Grisham's family instilled in him a strong work ethic and a respect for education, despite their modest means. His father, a construction worker and cotton farmer, moved the family frequently in pursuit of work, exposing Grisham to the struggles of working-class families. His mother, a homemaker, encouraged his love of reading and instilled in him the importance of learning. These values shaped his character and laid the groundwork for his future success, both as a lawyer and a writer.

It's important to note that Mississippi in the 1960s was also a place of rich storytelling traditions. From blues music to Southern Gothic literature, the state had a deep well of narratives that explored the human condition in all its complexity. Grisham was exposed to these influences, which likely contributed to his own ability to craft compelling stories that resonate with readers on an emotional level.

Grisham's early life in Mississippi was a melting pot of experiences that shaped his worldview and informed his perspective on justice. The social and cultural environment of his childhood, with its stark contrasts and inherent contradictions, provided fertile ground for the themes he would later explore in his writing. The seeds of his future career as a novelist and advocate were sown in the Mississippi soil, where he witnessed firsthand the power of storytelling and the urgent need for justice.

Family Background and Education

While the social and cultural landscape of Mississippi undoubtedly played a role in shaping John Grisham's worldview, his family background and education were equally influential in his journey to becoming a literary powerhouse and advocate for justice. Though his parents, Wanda and John Grisham Sr., may not have had extensive formal education, they instilled in their children the values of hard work, perseverance, and a deep respect for learning.

John Grisham Sr., a construction worker and cotton farmer, led a life marked by physical labor and the constant pursuit of employment opportunities. This itinerant lifestyle exposed young Grisham to the realities of working-class families across the South, fostering in him an understanding of their struggles and aspirations.

His father's dedication to providing for his family, even in the face of economic uncertainty, instilled in Grisham a strong work ethic that would serve him well in his future endeavors.

Wanda Grisham, a homemaker, played a pivotal role in nurturing Grisham's intellectual curiosity. Recognizing the importance of education, she encouraged her son's love of reading and instilled in him a thirst for knowledge. She fostered his imagination and provided him with the tools he needed to excel academically, setting the stage for his future success.

The Grisham household, though modest, was rich in love and support. John's parents, despite their limited resources, prioritized their children's education. They encouraged their sons to pursue higher education, a path that would eventually lead John to law school and ultimately to his career as a writer.

Grisham's parents, though not directly involved in the legal profession, instilled in him a strong moral compass and a sense of fairness. These values, coupled with his exposure to the inequalities of the South, ignited in him a passion for justice that would later become a defining characteristic of his writing.

It's fascinating to consider how the contrasting influences of his parents' professions shaped Grisham's aspirations. His father's blue-collar background provided him with a grounded understanding of the struggles faced by ordinary people, while his mother's emphasis on education opened up a world of intellectual possibilities. This unique blend of influences contributed to his multifaceted perspective and his ability to connect with readers from all walks of life.

Early Exposure to Law and Literature

John Grisham's journey to becoming a master storyteller wasn't solely shaped by his Southern upbringing and family values. It was also profoundly influenced by his early exposure to the worlds of law and literature, two seemingly disparate fields that would eventually converge in his writing.

Even before embarking on his legal career, Grisham was an avid reader, immersing himself in the works of literary giants. He found inspiration in the straightforward prose of John Steinbeck, appreciating the author's ability to convey complex emotions and social realities through clear and concise language. This influence is evident in Grisham's own writing style, which is characterized by its directness, accessibility, and focus on narrative drive.

Another significant literary influence was John le Carré, the master of spy fiction. Le Carré's intricate plots, morally ambiguous characters, and exploration of themes of betrayal and deception captivated Grisham. While his own novels delve into the legal world rather than espionage, the influence of Le Carré can be seen in Grisham's skillful plotting, his creation of suspenseful narratives, and his examination of the gray areas of morality within systems of power.

Grisham's early exposure to law, though indirect, also played a crucial role in shaping his future writing. He initially pursued a degree in accounting, but a chance encounter with a law student sparked his interest in the legal profession.

This newfound fascination led him to enroll in law school at the University of Mississippi, where he immersed himself in the intricacies of the legal system.

During his time in law school, Grisham developed a deep understanding of legal principles, courtroom procedures, and the nuances of legal arguments. He also witnessed firsthand the human drama that unfolded within the courtroom walls, observing the interplay between lawyers, judges, and juries. These experiences provided him with a wealth of material that would later inform his fiction, lending authenticity and depth to his portrayal of the legal world.

His early legal experiences weren't limited to the classroom. After graduating from law school, Grisham practiced criminal law in Southaven, Mississippi, for nearly a decade. He represented clients from all walks of life, gaining firsthand experience with the complexities of the legal system and the challenges faced by those seeking justice. He witnessed the devastating consequences of wrongful convictions, the power imbalances between individuals and corporations, and the ethical dilemmas faced by legal professionals. These real-life encounters with the flaws and injustices of the legal system fueled his desire to expose these issues through his writing.

CHAPTER 2:

THE PATH TO LAW

John Grisham's path to becoming a lawyer was far from linear, marked by a blend of ambition, happenstance, and a gradual realization that the courtroom, rather than the baseball diamond, was his true calling.

Pursuing a Legal Career

Initially, Grisham harbored dreams of a career in professional baseball. A talented player in his youth, he envisioned himself rising through the ranks to achieve Major League stardom. However, as he matured, he recognized the limitations of his athletic abilities and the fierce competition in the world of professional sports. This realization, coupled with a growing interest in intellectual pursuits, prompted him to shift his focus towards academia.

He initially pursued a degree in accounting, a practical choice that seemed to promise financial stability. But fate intervened in the form of a chance encounter with a law student who extolled the virtues of a legal career. Intrigued by the prospect of intellectual challenges and the opportunity to make a difference in people's lives, Grisham decided to take the plunge and enroll in law school at the University of Mississippi.

Law school presented its own set of challenges. The rigorous coursework, demanding professors, and competitive environment pushed Grisham to his limits. He had to adapt to a new way of thinking, mastering the art of legal analysis, argumentation, and research. But he persevered, driven by his newfound passion for the law and his determination to succeed.

During his law school years, Grisham's interest in criminal law blossomed. He was drawn to the high stakes, the human drama, and the opportunity to advocate for those accused of crimes. He also became increasingly aware of the flaws in the legal system, witnessing firsthand the disparities in access to justice and the potential for wrongful convictions. These experiences would later form the bedrock of his writing, fueling his desire to expose the injustices he observed.

Experiences as a Young Lawyer

After graduating from law school in 1981, Grisham returned to his hometown of Southaven, Mississippi, to embark on his legal career. He established his own practice, focusing primarily on criminal defense and personal injury cases. These early years as a young lawyer provided him with invaluable experience, exposing him to the realities of the courtroom and the complexities of the legal system.

One of the most significant cases Grisham handled during this period involved a young girl who had been brutally assaulted. The case deeply affected him, highlighting the devastating impact of crime on victims and their families. It also exposed him to the limitations of the legal system in providing true justice and healing. This experience would later serve as inspiration for his first novel, "A Time to Kill," which explored themes of racial injustice and vigilante justice.

Another case that left a lasting impression on Grisham involved a local family embroiled in a land dispute with a powerful corporation. He witnessed firsthand the tactics employed by large companies to intimidate and exploit individuals, further solidifying his understanding of the power imbalances that often exist within the legal system. This experience would later inform his portrayal of corporate malfeasance in novels such as "The Firm" and "The Pelican Brief."

Grisham's experiences in the courtroom weren't limited to high-profile cases. He also handled a wide range of everyday legal matters, from traffic violations to divorces. These seemingly mundane cases provided him with valuable insights into the human condition, exposing him to the struggles, hopes, and disappointments of ordinary people navigating the legal system.

His time as a lawyer also shaped his understanding of justice. He came to realize that justice wasn't always black and white, that the legal system was often fraught with complexities and ambiguities. He witnessed the impact of factors such as race, class, and social status on legal outcomes, and he grappled with the ethical dilemmas faced by legal professionals. These insights would later inform his nuanced portrayal of justice in his novels, where he often explored the gray areas of morality and the challenges of achieving true fairness.

The Impact of Real Cases on Grisham's Writing

Grisham's legal career provided him with a wealth of material that would later fuel his writing. He drew inspiration from real-life cases, incorporating elements of actual legal disputes, courtroom procedures, and legal strategies into his fictional narratives. This approach lent authenticity and depth to his stories, allowing him to explore complex legal issues within the framework of engaging narratives.

One of the most notable examples of this is his first novel, "A Time to Kill," which was inspired by a real-life case he witnessed in the courtroom. The novel tells the story of a Black man who takes the law into his own hands after his daughter is brutally assaulted, raising questions about race, justice, and the limits of the legal system. Grisham's firsthand experience with the case allowed him to capture the raw emotions and complex legal issues involved, creating a powerful and thought-provoking story.

Another example is "The Firm," which drew inspiration from Grisham's observations of the high-pressure world of corporate law firms. The novel follows a young lawyer who discovers that his prestigious firm is involved in illegal activities, forcing him to make difficult choices to protect himself and his family. Grisham's understanding of the inner workings of law firms, gained through his own experiences and observations, allowed him to create a believable and suspenseful narrative that resonated with readers.

Grisham's ability to weave real-life legal issues into his fiction is a hallmark of his writing. He doesn't shy away from tackling complex legal concepts, but he presents them in a way that is accessible and engaging to readers. He uses his legal expertise to craft believable scenarios, create compelling characters, and explore the human impact of legal disputes. This approach has earned him a loyal following among readers who appreciate his ability to entertain and inform simultaneously.

By drawing on his legal background, Grisham has been able to create a body of work that is both entertaining and insightful. His novels offer readers a glimpse into the inner workings of the legal system, exposing its flaws and celebrating its triumphs. They also raise important questions about justice, morality, and the human condition, prompting readers to think critically about the world around them.

CHAPTER 3:

THE BIRTH OF A BESTSELLING AUTHOR

John Grisham's transformation from a small-town lawyer to a literary phenomenon is a testament to his perseverance, his keen understanding of the human psyche, and his ability to tap into the zeitgeist with stories that resonate deeply with readers. His journey to becoming a bestselling author began with a spark of inspiration, a hefty dose of determination, and a story that refused to be ignored.

Writing "A Time to Kill"

The seed for Grisham's debut novel, "A Time to Kill," was sown in the courtroom. As a young lawyer, he witnessed the harrowing testimony of a 12-year-old girl who had been brutally assaulted. The experience shook him to his core and ignited within him a burning question: What if the victim's father had taken the law into his own hands? This question became the driving force behind "A Time to Kill," a story that explores themes of racial injustice, revenge, and the complexities of the legal system in the Deep South.

Grisham began writing "A Time to Kill" in 1984, dedicating his early mornings to the project before heading to his law office. He poured his heart and soul into the novel, drawing inspiration from his own experiences as a lawyer and his observations of the social and legal landscape of Mississippi. He completed the manuscript in three years, fueled by a passion to tell a story that would expose the injustices he witnessed and challenge readers to confront difficult questions about race, justice, and morality.

However, Grisham's path to publication was far from smooth. He faced numerous rejections from publishers who deemed the novel too controversial or regional in its appeal. Undeterred, he eventually secured a small publishing deal with Wynwood Press, which printed a modest 5,000 copies in 1989. Despite the limited print run, "A Time to Kill" garnered positive reviews and gradually gained traction among readers.

Navigating the Publishing World

The turning point in Grisham's career came with his second novel, "The Firm." This legal thriller, which tells the story of a young lawyer who discovers that his prestigious firm is involved in illegal activities, captured the attention of readers and critics alike. Published by Doubleday in 1991, "The Firm" quickly climbed the bestseller lists, establishing Grisham as a major force in the literary world.

The success of "The Firm" catapulted Grisham to international fame and opened doors to new opportunities. He became a sought-after speaker, a media personality, and a Hollywood favorite. His novels were adapted into blockbuster films, further amplifying his reach and solidifying his status as a cultural icon.

Grisham's transition from an unknown author to a bestselling novelist was fueled by a combination of factors. His legal background lent authenticity and credibility to his stories, while his innate storytelling abilities captivated readers with suspenseful plots and compelling characters. He also benefited from the growing popularity of the legal thriller genre, which tapped into public fascination with the law and its intricacies.

But Grisham's success wasn't solely due to luck or timing. He was a savvy marketer who understood the importance of connecting with readers. He embarked on extensive book tours, engaging with audiences and building a loyal fan base. He also cultivated relationships with booksellers and librarians, ensuring that his books were prominently displayed and readily available to readers.

The Success of "The Firm" and Its Aftermath

"The Firm" marked a significant turning point in Grisham's career, transforming him from a promising newcomer to a literary superstar. The novel's success allowed him to leave his law practice and devote himself entirely to writing. It also provided him with the financial security to pursue his passion projects, including his advocacy work for the wrongfully convicted.

The impact of "The Firm" extended beyond Grisham's personal career. The novel's popularity fueled a resurgence of interest in legal thrillers, inspiring a new generation of writers to explore the genre. It also solidified Grisham's reputation as a master storyteller who could weave complex legal issues into gripping narratives that resonated with readers from all walks of life.

The success of "The Firm" also paved the way for a series of successful film adaptations. The 1993 film adaptation, starring Tom Cruise, became a box office hit, further amplifying the novel's reach and introducing Grisham's work to a wider audience. This success led to a string of film adaptations of his other novels, including "The Pelican Brief," "A Time to Kill," and "The Client," solidifying his status as a Hollywood favorite.

The success of "The Firm" and its subsequent adaptations had a profound impact on Grisham's career trajectory. It allowed him to establish himself as a major force in the literary world, a bestselling author whose novels consistently topped the charts. It also provided him with the platform and resources to pursue his passion for justice, using his fame and influence to advocate for the wrongfully convicted and to raise awareness about the flaws in the legal system.

The legacy of "The Firm" continues to this day. The novel remains a popular read, and its film adaptation is considered a classic of the legal thriller genre. Grisham's subsequent works have also achieved remarkable success, solidifying his status as one of the most prolific and beloved authors of our time. His ability to weave compelling narratives that explore the complexities of the legal system, coupled with his unwavering commitment to justice, has earned him a loyal following among readers who appreciate his unique blend of entertainment and social commentary.

CHAPTER 4:

THEMES OF JUSTICE AND INJUSTICE

"Justice has nothing to do with what goes on in a courtroom; justice is what comes out of a courtroom." - John Grisham

This quote from Grisham himself encapsulates a core theme that resonates throughout his extensive body of work: the pursuit of justice, often in stark contrast to the very legal system designed to uphold it. His novels are not merely legal thrillers; they are morality tales, social commentaries, and explorations of the human condition in the face of injustice.

Recurring Motifs: More Than Just Legal Thrillers

Grisham's novels are populated with recurring motifs that reflect broader societal issues, anxieties, and struggles. These themes, often intertwined with intricate plots and compelling characters, elevate his work beyond simple genre fiction and contribute to their lasting impact on readers.

The David and Goliath Struggle: A common thread in many of Grisham's novels is the portrayal of ordinary individuals pitted against powerful adversaries. Whether it's a young lawyer taking on a corrupt law firm in "The Firm" or a small-town attorney fighting a ruthless corporation in "A Painted House," Grisham's protagonists often find themselves facing seemingly insurmountable odds. This motif resonates with readers because it taps into the universal fear of powerlessness in the face of large institutions and systemic corruption.

The Corruption of Power: Grisham's novels frequently expose the dark underbelly of power, whether it's wielded by corporations, government agencies, or individuals within the legal system itself. He portrays judges who bend the law to favor the wealthy, lawyers who prioritize profit over justice, and corporations that exploit loopholes to evade accountability. This recurring motif reflects a deep-seated societal concern about the abuse of power and the erosion of trust in institutions meant to serve the public good.

The Price of Greed: Many of Grisham's stories delve into the consequences of unchecked greed, often highlighting the devastating impact on individuals and communities. From the ruthless pursuit of profit in "The Rainmaker" to the environmental destruction depicted in "Sycamore Row," Grisham exposes the human cost of prioritizing financial gain over ethical considerations. This theme resonates with readers who are increasingly aware of the social and environmental consequences of corporate greed and economic inequality.

Redemption and Second Chances: Despite the often bleak scenarios depicted in his novels, Grisham also offers glimpses of hope and redemption. His protagonists, though flawed and vulnerable, often find the courage to fight for what's right, even when it means risking their careers or personal safety. This recurring motif reflects a belief in the human capacity for change and the possibility of finding justice, even in a flawed system.

Exploration of Wrongful Convictions: A Moral Imperative

Grisham's commitment to exposing the issue of wrongful convictions goes beyond his fiction. He has actively campaigned for criminal justice reform, using his platform to raise awareness and advocate for the wrongly accused. This dedication stems from a deep-seated belief that the justice system, while designed to protect the innocent, can sometimes fail spectacularly.

In his nonfiction book, "The Innocent Man," Grisham delves into the true story of Ron Williamson, a man wrongly convicted of murder and sentenced to death row. Through meticulous research and compelling storytelling, Grisham exposes the flaws in the investigation, the prosecutorial misconduct, and the systemic failures that led to Williamson's wrongful conviction. This book serves as a powerful indictment of a system that can sometimes prioritize expediency over truth and highlights the devastating consequences of wrongful imprisonment.

Grisham's fictional works also explore the theme of wrongful convictions, often showcasing the human toll of such injustices. In "Sycamore Row," he revisits the fictional town of Clanton, Mississippi, where "A Time to Kill" was set, to tell the story of a man wrongly accused of murder. The novel delves into the complexities of race, class, and prejudice within the legal system, highlighting the challenges faced by those seeking to overturn wrongful convictions.

Through both his fiction and nonfiction, Grisham provides valuable insights into the consequences of wrongful convictions. He sheds light on the emotional trauma endured by those wrongly accused, the loss of freedom and opportunities, and the ripple effects on families and communities. He also exposes the systemic issues that contribute to wrongful convictions, such as flawed forensic evidence, coerced confessions, and inadequate legal representation.

The Role of the Legal System: A Critical Lens

Grisham's portrayal of the legal system is both nuanced and critical. He doesn't shy away from depicting its flaws and shortcomings, but he also acknowledges its potential for achieving justice. His novels often serve as cautionary tales, highlighting the dangers of unchecked power, corruption, and systemic biases within the legal profession.

In "The Pelican Brief," Grisham exposes the vulnerability of the legal system to manipulation by powerful interests. The novel follows a law student who uncovers a conspiracy involving the assassination of two Supreme Court justices, revealing the lengths to which those in power will go to protect their interests. This story serves as a reminder that the law can be a tool for both justice and injustice, depending on who wields it.

"The Rainmaker" offers a scathing critique of the insurance industry and its tactics to deny legitimate claims. The novel follows a young lawyer who takes on a powerful insurance company that refuses to pay for a life-saving operation for a terminally ill client. Grisham exposes the company's ruthless pursuit of profit over human life, highlighting the ethical dilemmas faced by lawyers who must navigate a system that often favors the wealthy and powerful.

Grisham's fictional narratives often highlight real systemic flaws within the legal system. He exposes the disparities in access to justice, the influence of money and politics on legal outcomes, and the challenges faced by those seeking to hold powerful entities accountable. His stories serve as a call for reform, urging readers to recognize the imperfections of the legal system and to demand greater transparency, accountability, and fairness.

By shedding light on the vulnerabilities of the legal system, Grisham encourages readers to become more informed and engaged citizens. He empowers them to question authority, demand justice, and advocate for a more equitable society where the law truly serves the interests of all, not just the privileged few.

CHAPTER 5:

ADVOCACY FOR THE WRONGFULLY CONVICTED

"It's amazing to me that we still have this many wrongful convictions, with the advent of DNA and all the forensic tools that are available to prosecutors and police. It's amazing that we're still making so many mistakes." - John Grisham

John Grisham's dedication to justice extends far beyond the pages of his novels. He is a passionate advocate for the wrongfully convicted, leveraging his fame and influence to shed light on the systemic flaws that lead to these injustices. His activism and philanthropy have made a tangible impact on the lives of individuals who have been unjustly imprisoned, and his work has helped to raise awareness about the urgent need for criminal justice reform.

Grisham's Activism and Philanthropy: A Voice for the Voiceless

Grisham's commitment to advocating for the wrongfully convicted is deeply rooted in his experiences as a lawyer and his understanding of the vulnerabilities of the legal system. He has witnessed firsthand the devastating consequences of wrongful convictions, not only for the individuals involved but also for their families and communities. This understanding has fueled his desire to use his platform to bring attention to these injustices and to fight for a more just and equitable system.

One of the key ways Grisham has supported criminal justice reform is through his involvement with the Innocence Project, a non-profit legal organization that works to exonerate wrongfully convicted individuals through DNA testing and to reform the criminal justice system to prevent future injustices. Grisham has served on the Innocence Project's board of directors for many years, providing guidance and support to the organization's efforts. He has also used his platform to raise awareness about the Innocence Project's work, encouraging public support and donations to help fund its vital mission.

In addition to his work with the Innocence Project, Grisham has supported various other initiatives and organizations dedicated to criminal justice reform. He has donated generously to organizations that provide legal representation to those who cannot afford it, and he has spoken out in support of policies that aim to reduce wrongful convictions and improve the fairness of the legal system. He has also used his writing to shed light on these issues, incorporating themes of wrongful convictions and legal reform into his novels and nonfiction works.

Grisham's platform as an author has been instrumental in raising awareness about wrongful convictions. His novels, which often feature protagonists who are falsely accused or who fight to exonerate the innocent, have introduced millions of readers to the realities of wrongful convictions and the systemic issues that contribute to them. His nonfiction work, "The Innocent Man," which tells the true story of Ron Williamson's wrongful conviction and exoneration, has further amplified this message, reaching a wide audience and sparking important conversations about the need for criminal justice reform.

Notable Cases: Inspiration and Action

Grisham's advocacy work has been deeply influenced by several notable cases of wrongful convictions. These cases have not only inspired his writing but have also fueled his determination to fight for justice and to prevent similar injustices from happening to others.

One of the most significant cases that has impacted Grisham's activism is the case of Ron Williamson, which he chronicled in "The Innocent Man." Williamson, a former minor league baseball player, was wrongly convicted of murder and spent over a decade on death row before being exonerated by DNA evidence. Grisham's investigation into Williamson's case exposed a series of flaws in the investigation and prosecution, including faulty eyewitness testimony, coerced confessions, and prosecutorial misconduct. This case solidified Grisham's understanding of the systemic issues that contribute to wrongful convictions and fueled his desire to advocate for reform.

Another case that has had a profound impact on Grisham is the case of the West Memphis Three, three teenagers who were wrongly convicted of the murders of three young boys in West Memphis, Arkansas. Grisham was deeply troubled by the lack of evidence against the teenagers and the reliance on coerced confessions and dubious forensic evidence in their convictions. He joined the chorus of voices calling for their release, and he contributed financially to their legal defense. The West Memphis Three were eventually released from prison after spending 18 years behind bars, but their case remains a stark reminder of the fallibility of the justice system and the devastating consequences of wrongful convictions.

Grisham has also been involved in the case of Curtis Flowers, a Mississippi man who was tried six times for the same crime, a quadruple murder. Flowers, who is Black, was prosecuted by a white district attorney who was accused of racial bias in his jury selection. Grisham was appalled by the repeated trials and the apparent racial discrimination in the case, and he spoke out in support of Flowers's innocence. The case was eventually overturned by the U.S. Supreme Court, but it highlights the ongoing challenges of racial bias in the criminal justice system.

In each of these cases, Grisham has not only raised awareness about the injustices involved but has also actively collaborated with individuals and organizations working on these cases. He has provided financial support, legal expertise, and public advocacy to help secure the release of wrongfully convicted individuals and to bring attention to the systemic issues that contribute to these injustices.

Collaborations and Outcomes: The Power of Partnership

Grisham's collaborations with legal organizations, particularly the Innocence Project, have been instrumental in achieving tangible outcomes in the fight against wrongful convictions. These partnerships have combined Grisham's platform and resources with the legal expertise and advocacy power of organizations dedicated to criminal justice reform.

The Innocence Project, with Grisham's support, has helped to exonerate hundreds of wrongfully convicted individuals through DNA testing and legal advocacy. The organization has also been instrumental in pushing for reforms to prevent future wrongful convictions, such as improving eyewitness identification procedures, ensuring access to post-conviction DNA testing, and providing adequate legal representation for indigent defendants.

Grisham's involvement with the Innocence Project has not only helped to raise awareness about the issue of wrongful convictions but has also contributed to concrete changes in the legal system. His support has helped to fund the organization's vital work, and his public advocacy has helped to bring attention to the need for reform.

Grisham's collaborations with other legal organizations have also yielded positive results. He has worked with the Equal Justice Initiative, an organization that provides legal representation to those on death row and challenges racial and economic injustice in the criminal justice system. He has also supported the Center on Wrongful Convictions, which provides legal assistance to wrongfully convicted individuals and advocates for policy changes to prevent future injustices.

These collaborations have not only helped to secure the release of wrongfully convicted individuals but have also contributed to broader systemic changes. They have helped to raise awareness about the prevalence of wrongful convictions, the contributing factors, and the urgent need for reform. They have also helped to build momentum for policy changes that aim to improve the fairness and accuracy of the criminal justice system.

Grisham's real-world experiences with wrongful convictions and his collaborations with legal organizations have deeply informed his writing. His novels often feature characters who are falsely accused or who fight to exonerate the innocent, reflecting his understanding of the human toll of these injustices. His nonfiction work, "The Innocent Man," provides a detailed account of the systemic failures that can lead to wrongful convictions, drawing on his own experiences and research.

By integrating these real-world experiences into his writing, Grisham has been able to create a body of work that is both entertaining and socially relevant. His novels not only provide readers with thrilling narratives but also raise important questions about justice, fairness, and the human condition. They serve as a reminder of the fallibility of the legal system and the importance of fighting for the rights of all, especially those who have been marginalized or unjustly accused.

CHAPTER 6:

THE CRAFT OF STORYTELLING

"The key to writing is to write, not to study writing." - *John Grisham*

John Grisham's ability to craft compelling narratives that seamlessly blend legal complexities with gripping suspense is a testament to his unique approach to storytelling. His writing process, honed over decades, is a combination of discipline, meticulous research, and an innate understanding of human nature.

Grisham's Writing Process and Style: A Masterclass in Storytelling

Grisham's writing process is characterized by a disciplined and methodical approach. He typically begins each year with a new project, setting aside dedicated time each day to write. His writing routine is almost ritualistic, starting early in the morning in a quiet space free from distractions. He sets daily word count goals, pushing himself to maintain momentum and complete his manuscripts within a set timeframe.

This disciplined approach is reflected in Grisham's writing style, which is known for its clarity, conciseness, and focus on narrative drive. He avoids unnecessary flourishes or stylistic embellishments, prioritizing the story's flow and the reader's engagement. His prose is direct and accessible, allowing readers to easily immerse themselves in the narrative and follow the twists and turns of the plot.

Over time, Grisham's style has evolved, reflecting his growth as a writer and his exploration of different genres. While his early novels were primarily legal thrillers, he has since branched out into other areas, including sports fiction, political thrillers, and even a legal drama series for television. This diversification has allowed him to experiment with different narrative techniques and explore a wider range of themes and characters.

Despite these forays into new genres, Grisham's core writing style remains consistent. He maintains his commitment to clear and concise prose, compelling characters, and suspenseful plots that keep readers on the edge of their seats. He also continues to draw on his legal background, incorporating legal principles and courtroom procedures into his narratives to lend authenticity and depth to his storytelling.

Balancing Fiction with Real-Life Issues: The Art of Authenticity

One of Grisham's greatest strengths as a writer is his ability to balance fictional narratives with real-life issues. He seamlessly weaves complex legal concepts and social concerns into his stories, creating narratives that are both entertaining and thought-provoking. This ability to ground his fiction in reality is a key factor in his widespread appeal and his enduring popularity.

To ensure his fictional narratives remain grounded in reality, Grisham draws on his extensive legal background and his keen observation of the world around him. He meticulously researches legal principles, courtroom procedures, and the nuances of the legal profession to create believable scenarios and authentic characters.

He also incorporates real-life events and social issues into his stories, exploring themes of injustice, corruption, and the struggle for equality.

Grisham's ability to address complex legal issues without overwhelming readers is another hallmark of his writing. He avoids bogging down his narratives with technical jargon or legal minutiae, instead focusing on the human impact of legal disputes and the emotional stakes involved. He uses clear and concise language to explain legal concepts, making them accessible to readers without sacrificing accuracy or authenticity.

This delicate balance between fiction and reality is evident in many of Grisham's novels. In "The Firm," he explores the high-pressure world of corporate law firms, exposing the ethical dilemmas faced by young lawyers who are tempted by wealth and power. In "A Time to Kill," he tackles the complex issue of racial injustice in the Deep South, examining the legal and moral implications of vigilante justice. And in "The Innocent Man," he delves into the true story of Ron Williamson's wrongful conviction, exposing the flaws in the criminal justice system and the devastating consequences of wrongful imprisonment.

The Influence of His Legal Background: From Courtroom to Page

Grisham's legal training has had a profound influence on his narrative craft. His understanding of legal principles, courtroom procedures, and the adversarial nature of the legal system informs his plotting, character development, and thematic exploration. This legal lens adds a layer of authenticity and depth to his storytelling, allowing him to create narratives that are both credible and compelling.

One of the most evident ways Grisham's legal background enhances his storytelling is in his ability to craft believable legal scenarios.

He draws on his knowledge of legal precedents, courtroom etiquette, and the strategies employed by lawyers to create realistic and suspenseful courtroom scenes.

He also incorporates legal principles and procedural rules into his plots, adding a layer of complexity and intrigue to his narratives.

For example, in "The Pelican Brief," Grisham's understanding of environmental law and the workings of the Supreme Court allows him to create a credible conspiracy involving the assassination of two justices.

In "The Firm," his knowledge of corporate law and the ethical challenges faced by lawyers informs his portrayal of a young lawyer who discovers his firm's involvement in illegal activities. And in "A Time to Kill," his experience with criminal law and courtroom procedures allows him to craft a powerful and authentic portrayal of a racially charged murder trial.

Grisham's legal training also influences his character development.

He creates characters who are not only believable as legal professionals but also complex and multifaceted individuals with their own motivations, flaws, and vulnerabilities.

He draws on his observations of lawyers, judges, and clients to create characters who are both relatable and intriguing.

Furthermore, Grisham's legal background informs his thematic exploration. His novels often delve into complex legal and ethical issues, such as wrongful convictions, corporate malfeasance, and the struggle for justice in a flawed system.

He uses his understanding of the law to explore these themes in a nuanced and thought-provoking manner, raising important questions about morality, accountability, and the human condition.

Ultimately, John Grisham's craft of storytelling is a unique blend of disciplined writing habits, meticulous research, and the invaluable influence of his legal background.

He has mastered the art of balancing fiction with real-life issues, creating narratives that are both entertaining and thought-provoking.

His ability to address complex legal issues without overwhelming readers, coupled with his authentic portrayal of the legal world, has solidified his position as a master storyteller and a leading voice in the legal thriller genre.

CHAPTER 7:

RECENT WORKS AND CONTINUED IMPACT

"The law has always been a source of fascination for me, not just as a lawyer but as a writer. It's a world filled with drama, conflict, and moral dilemmas, all the ingredients for a good story." - John Grisham

John Grisham's literary journey has been remarkable, marked by consistent evolution and an unwavering commitment to exploring the intricacies of the legal world and the fight for justice. Even after decades of writing, he continues to captivate readers with his insightful narratives and his ability to weave contemporary societal issues into compelling fiction.

Overview of Recent Publications, Including "Framed"

In recent years, Grisham has continued to produce a steady stream of novels that showcase his versatility as a writer and his enduring fascination with the law. He has explored new themes, experimented with different narrative styles, and even ventured into the realm of nonfiction with works that shed light on the injustices of the legal system.

One of his recent notable publications is "Framed," a legal thriller that delves into the world of wrongful convictions and the fight to expose corruption within the legal system. The novel follows the story of a young lawyer who becomes entangled in a conspiracy involving a powerful judge and a corrupt prosecutor.

As he investigates the case, he uncovers a web of deceit and manipulation that threatens to destroy his career and his life.

"Framed" is a quintessential Grisham novel, combining a suspenseful plot with complex legal issues and thought-provoking themes. It explores the vulnerabilities of the legal system to corruption and the devastating consequences of wrongful convictions. The novel also touches on contemporary societal issues such as racial bias, economic inequality, and the abuse of power.

"Framed" has been well-received by critics and readers alike, praised for its gripping plot, authentic portrayal of the legal world, and timely exploration of social issues. Critics have commended Grisham's ability to maintain suspense while addressing complex legal concepts in an accessible manner. Readers have praised the novel's fast-paced narrative, relatable characters, and thought-provoking themes.

The Evolution of Themes: Reflecting a Changing World

Grisham's themes have evolved over time, reflecting his growth as a writer and his engagement with contemporary societal issues. While his early novels primarily focused on legal thrillers with themes of individual justice and corporate malfeasance, his recent works have expanded to encompass broader social concerns, including racial injustice, environmental issues, and political corruption.

This evolution is evident in novels such as "Sycamore Row," which revisits the fictional town of Clanton, Mississippi, to explore the lingering legacy of racial prejudice and the fight for civil rights. In "Gray Mountain," Grisham tackles the issue of environmental destruction caused by coal mining, highlighting the devastating impact on communities and the challenges faced by those who seek to hold corporations accountable. And in "The Reckoning," he delves into the complexities of post-World War II America, exploring themes of guilt, redemption, and the search for truth.

Grisham's recent writings are also influenced by contemporary societal issues such as the rise of populism, the erosion of trust in institutions, and the increasing polarization of political discourse.

In "The Whistler," he explores the dark side of casino gambling and the corruption that can permeate the legal system. In "Camino Winds," he tackles the issue of hurricane relief fraud, highlighting the exploitation of vulnerable communities in the aftermath of natural disasters. And in "A Time for Mercy," he revisits the character of Jake Brigance from "A Time to Kill" to explore the complexities of capital punishment and the moral dilemmas faced by those who must make life-or-death decisions.

Ongoing Influence: A Literary and Legal Legacy

John Grisham's impact on the legal thriller genre is undeniable. He has helped to popularize the genre, inspiring a new generation of writers to explore the complexities of the law and the drama of the courtroom. His novels have also influenced popular culture, with numerous film adaptations bringing his stories to a wider audience.

Grisham's influence extends beyond the literary world. His advocacy work for the wrongfully convicted and his commitment to exposing the flaws in the legal system have earned him respect and admiration from legal professionals and activists alike.

He is seen as a champion for justice, a voice for the voiceless, and a force for positive change.

Readers perceive Grisham as more than just an author; they see him as an advocate for justice, a storyteller who uses his platform to shed light on important issues and inspire action.

His novels not only entertain but also educate, raising awareness about the vulnerabilities of the legal system and the need for reform.

His commitment to justice resonates with readers who share his concern for the wrongfully convicted and his desire for a more equitable society.

Grisham's ongoing influence in literature and law is a testament to his enduring appeal as a storyteller and his unwavering commitment to justice.

His novels continue to captivate readers, his advocacy work continues to make a difference, and his legacy as a writer and activist is sure to endure for generations to come.

CHAPTER 8:

LEGACY AND FUTURE DIRECTIONS

"There is no such thing as a perfect legal system. Every system will have its flaws, and it's our job to constantly strive to improve it." - John Grisham

John Grisham's impact on the literary world and the fight for justice is undeniable. He has not only entertained millions with his gripping legal thrillers but has also used his platform to raise awareness about critical issues and inspire action. As we reflect on his legacy and look ahead to his future endeavors, it's clear that his contributions will continue to resonate for years to come.

Reflection on Grisham's Contributions: A Literary and Social Impact

Grisham's impact on literature is profound. He has helped to revitalize the legal thriller genre, bringing it to new heights of popularity and critical acclaim.

His novels have not only entertained readers but have also sparked important conversations about justice, ethics, and the human condition. He has introduced millions to the intricacies of the legal system, exposing its flaws and celebrating its potential for achieving justice.

Scholars recognize Grisham's cultural significance, acknowledging his ability to capture the zeitgeist and reflect the anxieties and aspirations of contemporary society. His novels often touch on themes that resonate with readers, such as the struggle against corporate greed, the fight for civil rights, and the pursuit of justice in a flawed system. He has also been praised for his ability to make complex legal concepts accessible to a wide audience, contributing to a greater understanding of the law and its impact on society.

Grisham's contributions to the criminal justice system are equally significant. His advocacy work for the wrongfully convicted has helped to raise awareness about the prevalence of wrongful convictions and the systemic issues that contribute to them.

He has used his platform to advocate for reform, supporting organizations like the Innocence Project and speaking out against injustices.

His work has helped to bring about tangible changes in the legal system, including improved access to DNA testing, enhanced safeguards against false confessions, and greater scrutiny of prosecutorial misconduct.

The Impact on Readers and Society: A Catalyst for Change

Grisham's novels have had a profound impact on readers, sparking empathy and inspiring action. His stories often feature ordinary individuals who find themselves caught up in extraordinary circumstances, fighting for justice against powerful adversaries.

These narratives resonate with readers who identify with the struggles of the underdog and who believe in the power of individual action to effect change.

Grisham's exploration of themes of justice has also contributed to a shift in public perception regarding wrongful convictions.

His novels and nonfiction works have shed light on the fallibility of the justice system and the devastating consequences of wrongful imprisonment.

This increased awareness has led to greater public support for criminal justice reform and a growing demand for accountability and transparency within the legal system.

Grisham's advocacy work has also contributed to this shift in public perception.

His involvement with organizations like the Innocence Project and his outspoken support for the wrongfully convicted have helped to bring these issues to the forefront of public consciousness.

His efforts have helped to create a more informed and engaged citizenry, one that is more likely to question authority and demand justice for all.

What Lies Ahead: Continuing the Fight for Justice

John Grisham shows no signs of slowing down. He remains a prolific writer, with new novels and projects on the horizon. He continues to explore contemporary societal issues, weaving them into compelling narratives that entertain and inform. His recent works, such as "Sparring Partners" and "The Boys from Biloxi," demonstrate his ongoing commitment to tackling complex themes and pushing the boundaries of the legal thriller genre.

Grisham's future work is likely to be influenced by the evolving landscape of publishing and the ongoing fight for social justice. The rise of digital publishing and the increasing importance of social media are likely to shape how he connects with readers and promotes his work. The ongoing struggles for racial justice, environmental protection, and economic equality are likely to continue to inform his themes and inspire his narratives.

Grisham's commitment to justice remains unwavering. He continues to advocate for the wrongfully convicted, support organizations dedicated to criminal justice reform, and use his platform to raise awareness about critical issues. His future endeavors are likely to include further collaborations with legal organizations, speaking engagements, and philanthropic initiatives aimed at promoting justice and equality.

Ultimately, John Grisham's legacy is one of literary excellence and unwavering commitment to justice. He has left an indelible mark on the literary world, the criminal justice system, and the hearts and minds of readers worldwide. His contributions will continue to inspire and inform for generations to come, as he continues to write, advocate, and fight for a more just and equitable world.

82

CONCLUSION

John Grisham's journey from small-town lawyer to literary giant and champion of justice is a testament to the power of storytelling and the unwavering pursuit of truth. His life and work offer a compelling narrative of personal growth, social responsibility, and the enduring human quest for fairness and equality.

From his humble beginnings in the Mississippi Delta to his current status as a bestselling author and influential advocate, Grisham has consistently demonstrated a deep commitment to exposing the flaws in the legal system and giving a voice to the voiceless.

His novels, though fictional, are deeply rooted in the realities of the legal world, drawing inspiration from his own experiences as a lawyer and his observations of the human condition.

He has masterfully woven complex legal concepts and social issues into compelling narratives that entertain and enlighten, captivating millions of readers worldwide.

Grisham's legacy extends far beyond the realm of entertainment. He has used his platform to raise awareness about critical issues, such as wrongful convictions, racial injustice, and corporate malfeasance. His advocacy work has made a tangible impact on the lives of individuals who have been unjustly imprisoned, and his efforts have contributed to a greater public understanding of the need for criminal justice reform.

This biography has provided a comprehensive exploration of Grisham's life, work, and advocacy, shedding light on the key factors that have shaped his journey and his contributions to literature and society.

It has delved into his childhood experiences, his legal career, his writing process, and his unwavering commitment to justice. Through this exploration, we have gained a deeper understanding of Grisham as an individual, his motivations, his values, and his enduring impact on the world.

This biography also contributes to a broader understanding of the context of justice reform.

By tracing Grisham's evolution as an advocate and examining the real-life cases that have inspired his work, we have gained valuable insights into the systemic issues that plague the legal system.

His stories serve as a powerful reminder of the human cost of injustice and the urgent need for reform.

They also offer hope, demonstrating the power of individual action and collective advocacy to bring about positive change.

In conclusion, John Grisham's life and work stand as a testament to the power of storytelling to entertain, enlighten, and inspire action. He has left an indelible mark on the literary world and the fight for justice, and his legacy will continue to resonate for generations to come.

53 Unknown Facts About Legal Thriller Master John Grisham:

A Glimpse Behind the Gavel

John Grisham: the name is synonymous with legal thrillers, courtroom drama, and the fight for justice.

But beyond the best-selling novels and blockbuster movies lies a man of intriguing contrasts and hidden depths.

A former lawyer turned literary icon, Grisham's journey is as captivating as his stories. Prepare to be surprised, intrigued, and inspired as we unveil 53 unknown facts about the legal thriller master himself.

From his childhood dreams to his hidden talents, his personal convictions to his surprising hobbies, this collection offers a rare glimpse into the man behind the pen.

53 Unknown Facts About Legal Thriller Master John Grisham

{KEY TAKEAWAYS}

1. **Before Law School, He Studied Accounting:** Grisham initially pursued a degree in accounting before switching to law. Imagine the legal thrillers we might have missed out on!

2. **He Once Dreamed of a Baseball Career:** A talented baseball player in his youth, Grisham envisioned a future in the Major Leagues before realizing his true calling lay elsewhere.

3. **He Served in the Mississippi House of Representatives:** Before achieving literary fame, Grisham served as a Democrat in the Mississippi House of Representatives from 1983 to 1990.

4. **"A Time to Kill" Was Rejected by 28 Publishers:** Grisham's debut novel faced a slew of rejections before finally finding a home with Wynwood Press. Perseverance pays off!

5. **He Wrote "A Time to Kill" in the Early Mornings:** Grisham dedicated his early mornings to writing before heading to his law office, showcasing his dedication and discipline.

6. **He's a Baptist:** Grisham's faith has played a role in his life and occasionally surfaces in his novels.

7. **He's a Coffee Aficionado:** Grisham starts his day with a strong cup of coffee, fueling his writing sessions. Perhaps this explains his prolific output!

8. **He Owns a Bookstore:** Grisham and his wife own an independent bookstore in Oxford, Mississippi, called Square Books.

9. **He's a Fan of Southern Literature:** Grisham draws inspiration from Southern literary giants like William Faulkner and Flannery O'Connor.

10. **He's a Prolific Reader:** Grisham is an avid reader, devouring books across various genres.

11. **He's Written More Than Just Legal Thrillers:** Grisham has explored other genres, including sports fiction, political thrillers, and even a legal drama series for television.

12. **He's a Skilled Carpenter:** Grisham enjoys woodworking and has built furniture for his home.

13. **He's a Passionate Advocate for Literacy:** Grisham supports literacy programs and initiatives that promote reading and education.

14. **He's a Dedicated Philanthropist:** Grisham and his wife have established a charitable foundation that supports various causes, including education, literacy, and disaster relief.

15. **He's a Recipient of the Harper Lee Prize for Legal Fiction:** This prestigious award recognizes authors who have made significant contributions to legal literature.

16. **He's Sold Over 300 Million Books Worldwide:** Grisham's novels have achieved phenomenal success, captivating readers across the globe.

17. **He's Had Several of His Novels Adapted into Films:** Many of Grisham's bestsellers have been transformed into blockbuster movies, further expanding his reach and influence.

18. **He's a Private Person:** Despite his fame, Grisham values his privacy and prefers to keep a low profile.

19. **He's a Family Man:** Grisham is married to Renee Jones, and they have two children together.

20. **He's a Dog Lover:** Grisham is a proud owner of several dogs.

21. **He's a Frequent Traveler:** Grisham's travels often inspire settings and characters in his novels.

22. **He's a Collector of First Editions:** Grisham has a passion for collecting first editions of his favorite books.

23. **He's a Supporter of Independent Bookstores:** Grisham believes in the importance of supporting local bookstores and frequently visits them during his travels.

24. **He's a Vocal Critic of the Death Penalty:** Grisham's opposition to capital punishment is often reflected in his novels and advocacy work.

25. **He's a Strong Believer in Second Chances:** Grisham's belief in redemption is a recurring theme in his novels.

26. **He's a Master of Suspense:** Grisham's ability to create suspenseful narratives is a hallmark of his writing.

27. **He's a Keen Observer of Human Nature:** Grisham's characters are often complex and

flawed, reflecting his understanding of the human condition.

28. **He's a Defender of the Underdog:** Grisham's protagonists often fight for justice against powerful adversaries, resonating with readers who identify with the struggle against injustice.

29. **He's a Voice for the Voiceless:** Grisham's advocacy work gives a voice to those who have been marginalized or unjustly accused.

30. **He's a Force for Positive Change:** Grisham's work has contributed to a greater public awareness of the need for criminal justice reform.

31. **He Once Had a Near-Death Experience:** Grisham was involved in a serious car accident as a young man, an experience that shaped his perspective on life.

32. **He's a Former Little League Coach:** Grisham coached his son's Little League team, drawing on this experience in his novel "Calico Joe."

33. **He's a Fan of Country Music:** Grisham enjoys listening to country music, and it occasionally features in his novels.

34. **He's a Skilled Gardener:** Grisham enjoys spending time in his garden, cultivating flowers and vegetables.

35. **He's a Supporter of Environmental Causes:** Grisham's concern for the environment is reflected in some of his novels, such as "Gray Mountain."

36. **He's a History Buff:** Grisham's interest in history often informs his writing, particularly in novels like "Sycamore Row" and "The Reckoning."

37. **He's a Believer in the Importance of Education:** Grisham supports educational initiatives and believes in the power of education to transform lives.

38. **He's a Member of the American Academy of Arts and Letters:** This prestigious organization recognizes outstanding achievements in literature, music, and art.

39. **He's Received Honorary Degrees from Several Universities:** Grisham's contributions to literature and society have been recognized with honorary degrees from institutions such as Mississippi State University and the University of Mississippi.

40. **He's a Member of the Mississippi Bar Association:** Grisham maintains his license to practice law in Mississippi.

41. **He's a Former Member of the Board of Directors of the Mississippi Innocence Project:** Grisham has been actively involved in efforts to exonerate wrongfully convicted individuals in Mississippi.

42. He's a Supporter of the Innocence Network: This network of organizations across the United States is dedicated to providing legal assistance to the wrongfully convicted.

43. He's a Frequent Speaker at Legal Conferences and Events: Grisham often shares his insights on the law, justice, and writing at legal conferences and events.

44. He's a Strong Advocate for Access to Justice: Grisham believes that everyone should have access to quality legal representation, regardless of their financial means.

45. He's a Critic of Mandatory Minimum Sentencing Laws: Grisham believes that these laws contribute to mass incarceration and disproportionately impact minority communities.

46. He's a Supporter of Sentencing Reform: Grisham advocates for reforms that would reduce

reliance on incarceration and promote rehabilitation.

47. **He's a Believer in the Importance of Jury Trials:** Grisham views jury trials as a cornerstone of the American justice system.

48. **He's a Critic of Plea Bargaining:** Grisham believes that plea bargaining can lead to wrongful convictions and undermines the integrity of the legal system.

49. **He's a Supporter of Restorative Justice:** Grisham believes in approaches to justice that focus on repairing harm and restoring relationships rather than solely on punishment.

50. **He's a Proponent of Transparency in the Legal System:** Grisham advocates for greater transparency in court proceedings and access to public records.

51. **He's a Supporter of Legal Aid Organizations:** Grisham believes in the importance of providing legal assistance to those who cannot afford it.

52. **He's a Critic of the Influence of Money in Politics:** Grisham believes that the influence of money in politics undermines democracy and can lead to corruption.

53. **He's an Optimist About the Future of Justice:** Despite the challenges, Grisham remains optimistic that the legal system can be reformed to better serve the interests of justice and equality.

John Grisham's life is a testament to the power of pursuing one's passions, whether it's crafting gripping legal tales or fighting for the wrongfully convicted. These 53 facts reveal a man of diverse interests, unwavering principles, and a deep commitment to making a difference in the world. He is more than just a writer; he is a champion of justice, a voice for the voiceless, and an inspiration to those who believe in the power of words to effect change. As Grisham continues to write, advocate, and inspire, his legacy as a literary giant and a force for good will undoubtedly endure.

GRATITUDE AND A HUMBLE REQUEST

Thank you for reading *John Grisham Biography: Exploring the Framed Victims of a Flawed Legal System and the Craft of Justice*! I hope you found it insightful and engaging.

If you enjoyed this journey into the life and work of John Grisham, please consider leaving an honest review on Amazon. Your feedback helps other readers discover the book and learn how it might impact their lives. It also helps me grow as an author and produce even better work in the future.

Thank you for your support!

{Morris Glisson}

Printed in Dunstable, United Kingdom

65492269R00057